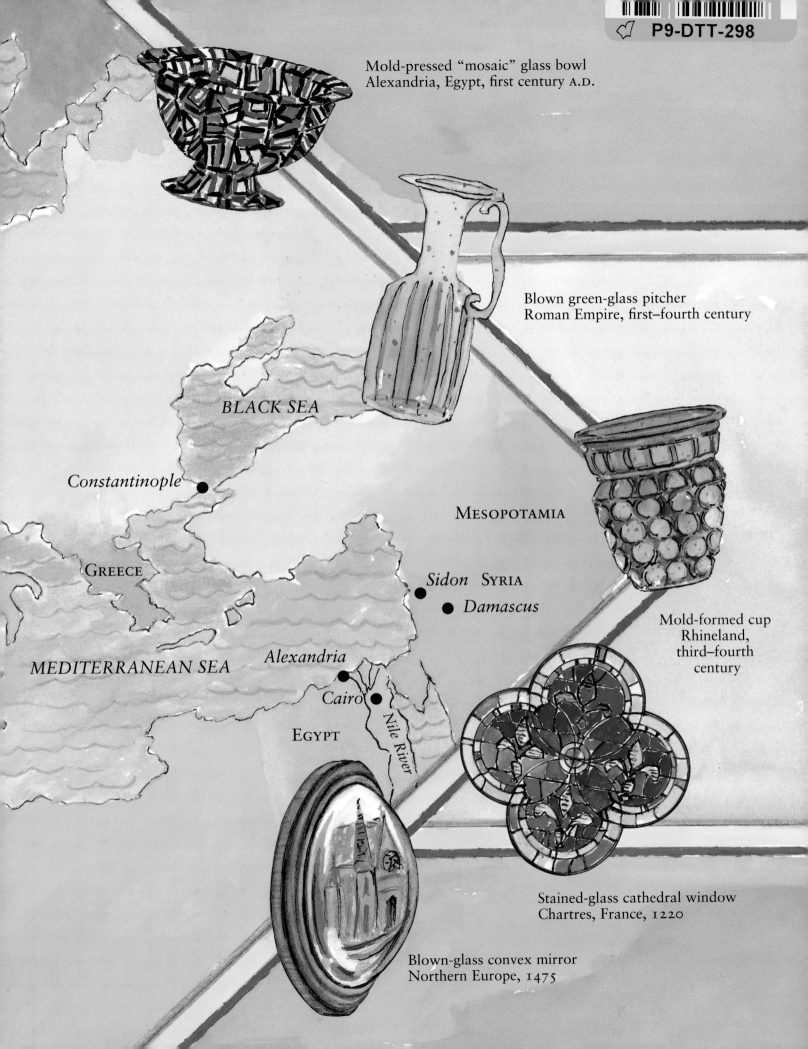

Mold-pressed "mosaic" glass bowl
Alexandria, Egypt, first century A.D.

Blown green-glass pitcher
Roman Empire, first–fourth century

BLACK SEA

Constantinople

MESOPOTAMIA

GREECE

Sidon SYRIA
Damascus

Mold-formed cup
Rhineland,
third–fourth
century

MEDITERRANEAN SEA

Alexandria

Cairo

EGYPT

Nile River

Stained-glass cathedral window
Chartres, France, 1220

Blown-glass convex mirror
Northern Europe, 1475

Looking at Glass Through the Ages

To Edwin and Irene

All rights reserved. For information about permission to reproduce
selections from this book, write to Permissions,
Houghton Mifflin Company, 215 Park Avenue South,
New York, New York 10003.

www.houghtonmifflinbooks.com

The text of this book is set in Sabon.
The illustrations are watercolor.

Library of Congress Cataloging-in-Publication Data
Koscielniak, Bruce. Looking at glass through the ages / by Bruce Koscielniak.
p. cm.
ISBN 0-618-50750-7 (hardcover)
1. Glass—History—Juvenile literature. I. Title.
TP849.K67 2006
666'.1—dc22
2005003916

ISBN-13: 978-0618-50750-4

Printed in Singapore
TWP 10 9 8 7 6 5 4 3 2 1

Looking at Glass
Through the Ages

BY BRUCE KOSCIELNIAK

Houghton Mifflin Company

Boston 2006

Glass. It's everywhere. It's our window on the world. It's likely to be the drinking glass, sugar bowl, or salt shaker on our dinner table. It's probably part of our wristwatch, our television, and our sunglasses, too. We couldn't get along without it.

But what exactly is this extraordinary material, and how did it come to be used in so many different ways? To find the origins of glass, we have to look back at least 4,500 years.

The blue-green color of faience was produced by the addition of ground copper to the glass mixture.

Faience necklace beads

Egyptian faience Shawabti figure, 2000 B.C. Figures were to perform tasks for the dead.

Before firing, faience was a thick paste that could be shaped by hand or pressed into a mold.

The earliest known glass, called *faience*, was produced by the Egyptians around 2500 B.C. in the form of beads, often deep blue or turquoise in color. Someone, either in Egypt or Mesopotamia, had discovered that oven-firing a mixture of silica sand (quartz being a common silica, and the major component of sand) with soda ash (sodium carbonate, made by burning plants or hardwood) would produce a bead or gob of material that was brittle and almost gemlike in appearance. The addition of soda ash to the sand allows the quartz to melt at a lower temperature. The Egyptians also added a little lime to strengthen the fired product. This was early glass.

By 1500 B.C., the Egyptians, who used many body lotions and oils, were making small glass containers for their makeup and ointments by coating a soft shaped core of clay and straw with molten glass, often dark blue. They then wrapped strands of heated glass around the glazed core, using bright colors such as red, yellow, and light blue, as well as white. The strands were combed into a decorative wave pattern, then rolled flat, and when the glass cooled and became rigid, the clay core was washed out.

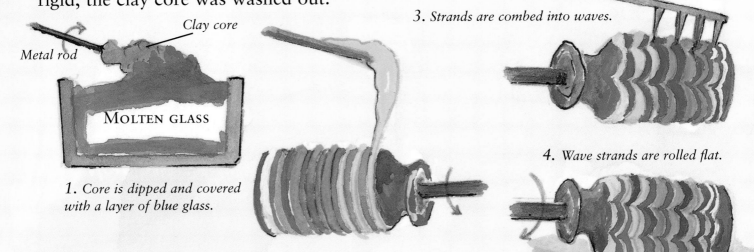

Clay core

Metal rod

MOLTEN GLASS

1. Core is dipped and covered with a layer of blue glass.

2. Colored glass strands are applied.

3. Strands are combed into waves.

4. Wave strands are rolled flat.

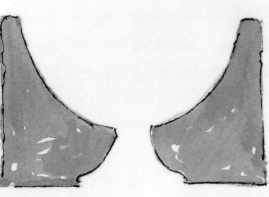

In Alexandria, Egypt, which was a center of glassmaking beginning around 330 B.C., a mold was used to form glass items. First, molten glass was pressed into a mold. After it cooled, the mold was taken apart and the piece was polished with abrasives. This process allowed larger, identically formed glass pieces to be made more quickly.

1. *Outer mold shell*

2. *Molten glass pieces set in mold*

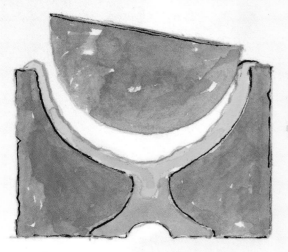

3. *Inner core pressed into hot glass*

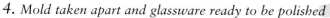

4. *Mold taken apart and glassware ready to be polished*

*Millefiore
or mosaic
"thousand flowers"
glass*

mosaic glass slices

Alexandria's glassmakers learned to combine different-colored molten-glass rods into thick cables that were then cut in cross sections to make patterned glass. The slices of glass would be pressed into a mold to produce a vessel with an overall multicolor mosaic look, or a "thousand flowers" pattern.

One of the most important discoveries in the history of glassmaking, thought to have been made around 30 B.C. in Sidon, Syria, was that a gob of molten glass on the end of a hollow metal tube could be blown into a bubble.

Glassblowers, also using a solid iron bar called a *pontil* or *punty,* a flat block of stone called a *marver,* and various shaping tools, could freely form the hot glass by hand, or they could simply blow the bubble into a mold.

SIDON BECAME PART OF THE
ROMAN EMPIRE IN 27 B.C.

Blowing iron (5 feet long)

Pontil

1. Bubble

2. Shaped on marver

3. Pontil is welded with glass to container bottom.

4. Blowpipe is cut off.

5. Neck and bottle lip can be reheated and finished, then pontil is cracked off.

6. Stems, bases, and handles are added separately.

Marver

With this innovation, glass production in the Roman world (first to fourth century A.D.) increased greatly and included luxury glass items as well as everyday-use green-tinted glass containers.

In the Middle Ages, after the division of the Roman Empire, Constantinople became a center of glassmaking knowledge, producing much-admired cut-glass pieces.

Cut-glass jar

CONSTANTINOPLE

Before the year 1250, most glass had been colored or tinted, because natural impurities in the glass mixture will tint the glass. Decolorizing additives had been used since Roman times, but it still wasn't fully known how to produce colorless transparent glass. In the fifteenth century, however, the glassmakers of Venice, Italy, were able to develop a fairly clear colorless glass called *cristallo,* which was made with a highly guarded formula and was unique to Venice.

VENICE

The Roman writer Seneca noticed that looking through a goblet of water could produce a magnifying effect.

In 1291, Venice's glass-making industry was moved to the nearby isle of Murano, to prevent fire in the city.

The Arabian scholar Alhazen was the first to study and write in detail about light and lenses, around A.D. 1000

1352 painting showing early use of spectacles.

The successful effort to produce clear colorless glass brought about the introduction of magnifying lenses and reading spectacles. An Italian fresco painting of 1352 depicts a pair of early magnifying spectacles worn by a scribe.

Lenses work because light passing through glass slows down and is "bent" to change direction. This is called *refraction*.

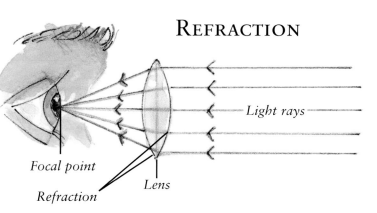

REFRACTION

Light rays

Focal point

Refraction

Lens

A magnifying lens gathers light and is shaped thicker at the center to bring the refracted light rays together at a focal point beyond the lens to produce the magnified image we see.

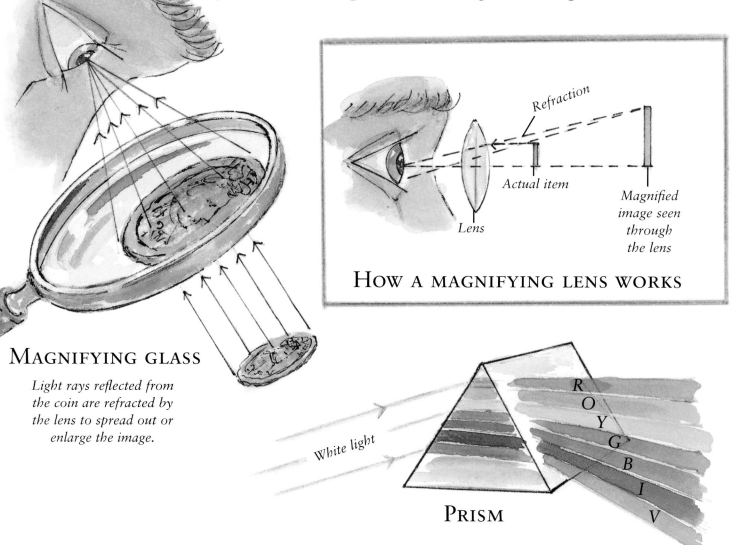

MAGNIFYING GLASS

Light rays reflected from the coin are refracted by the lens to spread out or enlarge the image.

Refraction

Actual item

Lens

Magnified image seen through the lens

HOW A MAGNIFYING LENS WORKS

White light

R
O
Y
G
B
I
V

PRISM

A prism is a triangle-shaped solid glass form that refracts white light (sunlight, for example) into its separate component colors—red, orange, yellow, green, blue, indigo, and violet, thus producing a rainbow of colored light.

Enameled beads

The Venetians also developed techniques in glass engraving (scratching a design into the glass with a pointed tool) and enameling to create a high art. Enamel is a glass-based paint that is kiln-fired to permanently fuse the color to the glass object. Enameled gold-paste-filled beads called *perle a lume* were a Venetian specialty in the 1400s.

In the twelfth and thirteenth centuries, glass took on a striking role in the form of stained-glass windows in the gothic cathedrals of Europe. The windows became works of art, painting stories from the Bible in colored light.

The crudely made glass that was used, with its ripples, bubbles, and uneven color density, was beautifully suited for cathedral windows. Colored glass is produced by the addition of metals or metal oxides (metals exposed to moist air will corrode to form oxides) to the glass mixture: cobalt for blue, iron for green, antimony for yellow, manganese for purple, and gold for deep ruby reds.

To make the stained-glass pieces, glassblowers would make a cylinder of glass, trim off the ends, and cut the tube lengthwise, so it could be reheated and flattened into a sheet of about ten by twelve inches and one-eighth to one-fourth inch thick.

Glassworks were located near the edges of forests because of the vast amounts of wood fuel needed.

MELTING CHAMBER
Fireclay pots hold a batch of glass

FUEL AND AIR FOR FIRE

A full-size drawing of the window, which showed all the pieces of glass and the color of each piece, was made. The drawing was divided into separate sections, or panels, and a panel drawing would be transferred (painted directly) onto a whitewashed worktable.

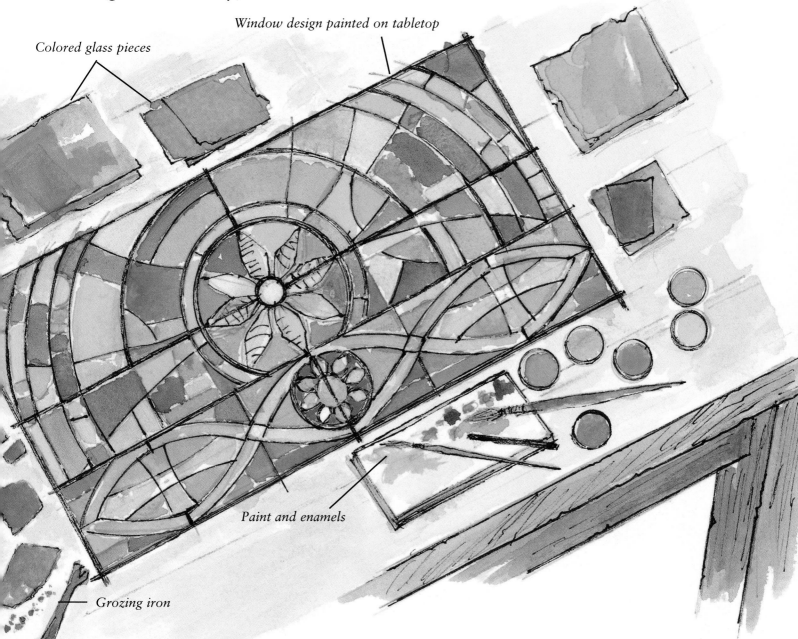

Window design painted on tabletop

Colored glass pieces

Paint and enamels

Grozing iron

The colored glass sheets were selected and shaped by running a red-hot iron over the cut line and cracking the glass along the heated line. Further shaping could be done by chipping the glass away with a notched tool called a *grozing iron*. If the design called for enameling, the pieces would be enameled and heated in a kiln.

The lead strips, called came,
were fastened with solder,
a metal alloy (mixture)
that melts at a low temperature.

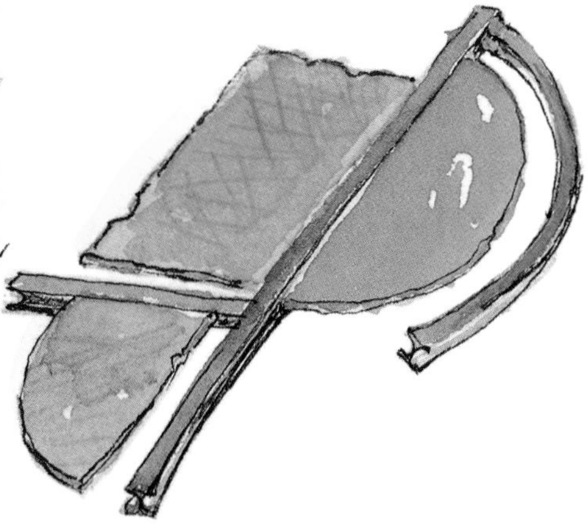

The glass pieces were then put together and held in place by grooved strips of lead. Completed panels were weatherproofed with putty and installed with an iron rod framework in the window opening in the building. The iron supports were made to work as part of the overall design. To this day, medieval stained-glass windows remain a magnificent achievement.

For many of us, one of the first things we may do in the morning is look in a mirror. In the ancient world, mirrors were made of highly polished metal. Glass mirrors, sometimes called *looking glasses,* came into use around the thirteenth century, and are made by "silvering," that is, coating the back of the glass with a thin reflective layer of tin, silver, or other metal. The glass provides a smooth, nonporous surface for the metal, which provides the reflection.

Convex mirrors were cut from blown-glass bubbles, and hot metal, often lead, was poured into the bowl, to thinly coat the back of the mirror.

Thin layer of tin, aluminum, or silver

Glass

Objects in a mirror appear in reverse or "mirror image." Objects also appear as distant behind a flat mirror as they are in front of the mirror.

Convex mirror (side view). Convex mirror image is smaller than the actual object.

Small convex (bulging at the center) blown-glass mirrors were commonly used from the thirteenth through the fifteenth centuries, and were frequently depicted in Flemish paintings of that time.

By the sixteenth century, Venetian glass shops were producing highly prized flat wall mirrors made of cristallo glass for use throughout Europe. These mirrors often had beveled edges and were set in ornately decorated frames.

In England and Ireland in the 1700s, lead oxide was an added ingredient used to make a brilliant colorless glass called *lead crystal*. This fairly soft high-contrast glass was often decorated with deeply cut diamond patterns that refract light to make the glass sparkle like a real polished gemstone. Cutting wheels of brass and wood covered with fine abrasives and oil were used to cut and buff the glassware.

Bottles and jars were
sealed with cork and
wax or metal foil.

Hinged mold, 1820

Glassmakers in England and America were able to give inexpensive, everyday-use bottles, jars, and inkwells a fancy cut-glass look simply by blowing or pressing bottle glass into a patterned mold. Common bottle glass, which usually had a greenish cast, could also be made in blue-greens, brown, or amber—colors produced by natural materials like iron in the glass mixtures, or by the addition of other coloring oxides.

Ever notice in an older building that the windows may have a rippled or dimpled surface that makes things appear wavy when you look through them? Before 1900 or so, window glass was difficult to produce. The old method of cutting and flattening a glass cylinder into sheet glass was still in use.

1. Blown cylinder is trimmed.

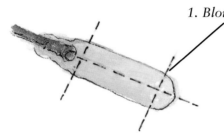

2. Hot glass is rolled flat.

3. Cooled glass is cut into panes.

"Bull's-eye" crown pieces could be smoothed and used for semitransparent windows.

Window glass was also made by the centuries-old practice of trimming the end off of a globe of molten glass, attaching a pontil, and spinning it rapidly so that the glass would form into a nearly flat disk. This is called *crown glass* because of the jagged crown left when the pontil was cracked off. The disk would then be cut into individual panes.

Today, machines do the work to produce hundreds of square yards of perfectly finished *sheet* or *plate glass* per hour, as well as all the other varied glass products we use. No ripples, bubbles, or dimples are included in the modern-day "float glass" process, in which glass is formed into large sheets by melting the ingredients and floating the soft flowing glass on a perfectly flat pool of molten tin. The molten glass is then slowly cooled and rolled off for cutting.

The float glass process was invented in the 1950s.

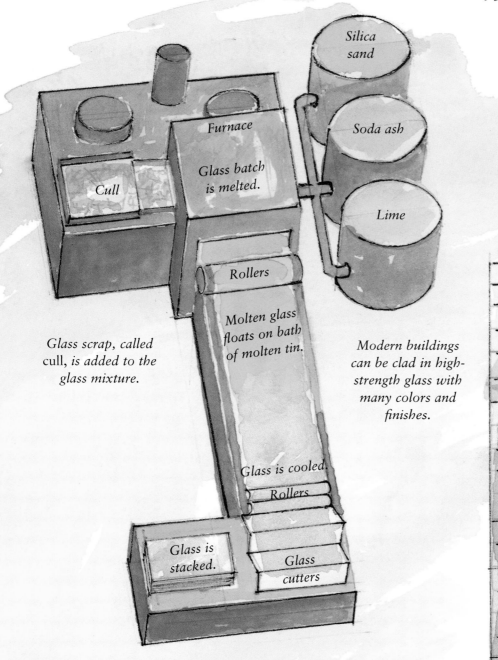

Silica sand

Soda ash

Lime

Furnace

Glass batch is melted.

Cull

Rollers

Molten glass floats on bath of molten tin.

Glass scrap, called cull, is added to the glass mixture.

Modern buildings can be clad in high-strength glass with many colors and finishes.

Glass is cooled.

Rollers

Glass is stacked.

Glass cutters

Modern molding methods use compressed air and press stamping to produce glass items from coffeemaker pots to auto headlamps.

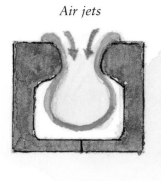

Air jets

Hot glass

Press mold

Headlamp lens

Changes to the basic glass mixture can produce many specialized types of glass for high-strength, optical, or high-technology uses. For example, heat-resistant ovenware is made with the addition of boric oxide to the silica.

Oven-safe glass

High-grade lenses are made of highly refined silica sand fused at a very high temperature of over 3,100 degrees Fahrenheit, making this one of the most expensive types of glass to produce.

Fused-silica telescope mirror

Although most of the glass products we use are machine made, glassmakers worldwide, working in small shops, often with gas-fired or electric heating units, continue to produce beautiful, functional, or purely decorative art glass pieces by hand.

Melting oven

Reheating oven, called the glory hole.

Marver bench

Pipes and pontil

Premixed ingredients for clear glass, simply called *soda glass,* can be purchased ready to use, in conveniently sized sacks. As in the past, the finely powdered mixture is poured into a fireclay pot and "cooked" for thirty hours or more at up to 2,600 degrees Fahrenheit to melt and to remove gas bubbles and other impurities, which are then skimmed off.

At working temperature, the glass batch, called *metal,* is about the consistency of honey. The glassmaker must work very quickly and continually reheat a piece of glass-work to an orange-yellow glow, because the glass will begin to harden in seconds.

A wide variety of preprepared colored glass is also available to today's glass-ware and stained-glass artists.

Stained-glass sample pieces

*Mold-blown,
color-layered glass bowl*

Colored glass layer

*Prepared, concentrated
colored glass is made in
the form of glass rods.*

Clear glass layer

Richly colored glass pieces are often made by fusing a thin film of colored glass to a heavier layer of clear glass. Frosted surface effects can be achieved by sandblasting the glass.

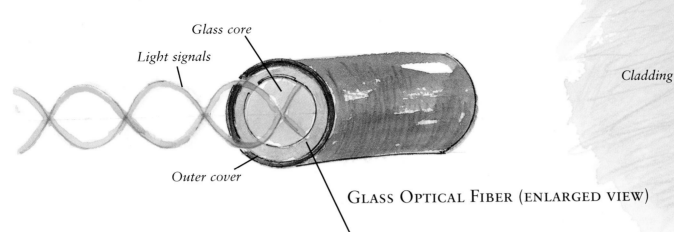

Glass core

Light signals

Outer cover

GLASS OPTICAL FIBER (ENLARGED VIEW)

Cladding

Core

Invented in 1970, glass optical fibers the thickness of human hairs can carry information around the world in the form of pulses of laser light.

Glass cladding, a layer of glass that reflects the light signals back into the core and keeps them moving along through the solid glass core in a process called total internal reflection. To travel long distances, light signals must be amplified at points along the way.

As a part of our new electronic gadget or in miles of glass optical fiber employed in worldwide communications systems; as a brightly colored neon sign or a handmade glass paperweight—the ways in which glass can be used are open to human inventiveness and the skill of glassmakers. The glassy material itself, opaque or transparent, continues to engage and fascinate us with its unique beauty.

Molten glass rod

Glass optical fibers are made by drawing a preformed layered molten glass rod downward and, when cooled, rolling it onto a spool.

For a neon sign, glass tubes are heated and bent to form letters, then filled with neon gas, which is energized by electricity to glow brightly.

Glass fiber cools

PIZZA

Glass is still made today from a process discovered 4,500 years ago—transforming ordinary sand, lime, and ash, as if by magic, into a most extraordinary material.